From Infinity To Infinity

Dijon Bowden

All rights reserved. No part of this publication may be reproduced, distributed, or transmitted in any form by any means, including photocopying, recording, or other electronic methods without the prior written permission of the author, except in the case of brief quotations embodied in reviews and certain other noncommercial uses permitted by copyright law. For permission requests, write to the author at the address below.

Dijon Bowden
www.dijonbowden.com

ISBN: 978-1-7352328-2-9

Printed in the United States of America
First Printing, 2020

Editing: Tell Tell Poetry | www.telltellpoetry.com
Interior Design: Cover&Layout | www.coverandlayout.com
Cover Design: Dijon Bowden | www.dijonbowden.com

DEDICATION

For my Mom, Alysha, and Kobe—
you were shelter from the storm

Contents

I   1

In the Light of Venus   3
The Stagnancy of My Sadness   4
Chinese Finger Cuffs   5
Swirling Angels   6
Life's Not Easy   7
The Key to the Next Dimension   8
Ubuntu   9
Sacred Silence   10
Puzzle Peace   11
Surrender   12
The Speed of Nature   13
God is Love   14
The Kite and the Rock   16
Inner Jewels   17
Heart-centered Living   18
The Jubilation of Self-realization   19
True Love Aligns   20
Cerebellum's Cage   21
Awaken with Grace   22
Pure Presence   23
Illusions   24
Faultline   25
Portals and Pathways   26

II   29

Fluorescent Waves   31
Arcturus   32
Spirits' Kiss   33
Essence   34

Ripe Fruit	35
Young Soul	36
A New Path	37
Sorrow's Sting	38
Virgin Snow	39
Let Go	40
Illumination	41
Devotion	42
Rainbow Muse	43
Law of Attraction	44
Russian Roulette	45
Ambrosia	46
Soul Science	47
A Field of Jasmine	48
Harmony	49

III 51

Reverence	53
Poppies and Lavender	54
Alchemy	56
Remembrance	57
Hungry Ghosts	58
Timeless Love	60
The Farmer and the Peach	61
Divine Vibrations	62
Discipline	63
Free from Sin	64
Distractions	65
Ancient Ancestors	66
The Rhythm of Flow	67
Unplug	68
Rejuvenation	69
Keys to Awakening	70

Astrally Attuned	71
Heavens' Gate	72
Smooth Sandpaper	73
Debt Free	74
Icarus	75
Your Child	76
Homecoming	78

IV — 81

Pollination	83
Lemurian Love	84
A New Start	86
The Universe Chose Us	87
Medjool Dates	88
Twin Flame	89
Conscious Creator	90
Blanket of Light	91
Celestial Captain	92
The Cosmic Ray	93
Balance Beam	94
Rebirth	95
The Womb	96
Astral Aviation	98
Sacred Ground	99
Floating Ships	100
Divine Decadence	101
Royalty	102
Selfless	103
Starseed	104
Tiny Totems	106
Oceanic Reflections	107
Under Moroccan Skies	108
About the Author	111

I

Dijon Bowden

In the Light of Venus

I dove into the darkness to witness myself.
I found jagged edges in need of sanding.
When I polished them, they started to shine.
I placed the primordial diamonds in my pocket and smiled.

In the light of Venus,
I climbed to the top of Cowles mountain
and looked out over the frontier.
Mist wafted over rolling green hills
while the sun tickled his peaks
and hid from her valleys.

In the light of Venus,
I saw butterflies dancing in the wind
with wings fluttering in fiery playfulness,
charging at each other
and then banking east together in perfect formation.

They're flying towards a dark valley,
staying synchronized
with equal parts sophistication and simplicity.
Their sapphire and cerulean wings glisten as they approach a peak
and cross over into the light of the sun.

The Stagnancy of My Sadness

The stagnancy of my sadness
invites me to surrender
the habitual indulgence of my pride, anger, and fear.

I clear away the debris
that blocks me from peace, love, joy, and harmony.
Success seduces me with a promise of solutions
but there is no end that denotes a resolute conclusion.

Life is a continuous exploration of the multi-dimensional *now*,
to be divinity embodied the *what*,
meditation and yoga the *how*.

Buried within is God's eternal, unconditionally loving presence.
As I venture beyond ego,
I discover the treasure of my indestructible cosmic essence.

Chinese Finger Cuffs

The Chinese finger cuffs snapped
and I finally broke free.

I realized step two comes before step three.
Loving you comes after loving me.

The first step is remembering that I am one with God,
that I actualize this truth with deed, word, and thought,

that I don't need a specific relationship to cultivate me
but also that, without a reflection, there's nothing to see.

It is up to me to embody my soul.
It is up to me to choose to feel whole.

What a dance we have tried to control.
Let's let go to spin free and embody life's only goal.

SWIRLING ANGELS

Uriel and Michael swirling in the mist,
protecting my orbit with ferocity,
giggling gleefully as they shout and twist,
accelerating my ascension with great velocity.

I am a chosen one
as I choose my Self.
Yeshua and Babaji make the same choice unceasingly
to expand upon their inner health.

The direction is always inward.
Trusting and investing in self
ripens your spirit like sweet grapes in a California vineyard,
elevated consciousness the greatest wealth.

LIFE'S NOT EASY

Life's not easy,
but it's incredibly simple.
You find the wave

when you tune into tempo.
The vibration is smooth, steady, and slow.
Trust the rhythm of life,

release,

let go.

The Key to the Next Dimension

The key to unlocking the next dimension is within me.

I'm dancing delightfully through the door to higher consciousness
with discipline, devotion, and consistency.

The gift of the present now reveals to me
dead-end temptations that distract me.

I choose now, and in every moment, to be
my radiant self,

shining like the blazing sun
over the endless sea,
unconditionally loving and eternally free.

Ubuntu

You've been playing small,
hiding,
avoiding what you know to be true.
And yet, you act as if God's been hiding from you.

The time has come to stand tall,
to elevate,
to see it all the way through,
look within to recall,
to integrate,
to embody Ubuntu.

Freedom awaits you now.
You can rise above this demented zoo.
Your family, ancestors, and spirit guides
are all here to support you.

Sacred Silence

Today is a day to rejoice
as I'm learning to love silence more than I like noise.

As much as I love expansion,
I'm learning to embrace contraction.
My preference is now Vedic meditation
instead of dancing with distraction.

In your eyes, I feel immense satisfaction
because I recognize you are a light refraction,
a divine mirror showing me my greatest wealth,
the beauty of my immortal, divine reflected self.

Puzzle Peace

Peace is perceiving the perfection in all things.
Joy is gratitude embodied.
Love replaces perception with vision.
Reason elevates lust to passion.
Acceptance is free from inner resistance.
Willingness welcomes all expressions of life.

When your pride is subject to obliteration
from your ego's annihilation,
your journey has just begun.

Surrender

I surrender my selfishness
so that my Self can lead the way.

In the darkness of the night,
the moon washes away the day.

The stars emit beams of light
till the sun illuminates the sky.

I watch the rapturous dance of bountiful butterflies,
transient, radiant rainbows capture cosmic essence,
fleeting phenomena covering unchanging loving presence.

In gratitude, I give thanks that I get to be
a mighty wave, rising as a unique expression of eternity.

Dijon Bowden

The Speed of Nature

It isn't love till you know someone's scars.
There may be sparks and stars.
We feel ready to bust, but we know lust
is just sex without TRUST.

There's no rush, I'm here.
I'm not in a hurry,
no expectations, pure presence.
Time will assuage all our worries.

Our love grows at the pace
of a Northern California redwood tree,
laying our hearts bare to reveal wounds
but not too soon.

We patiently share our souls,
hopes, dreams, and goals,
while we lie in a field, staring up at the moon.

There's no rush is what I keep saying.
Let's stay focused on God, purpose, and playing.

Whatever comes to be will be.
We'll always be friends.
I'm there for you
and you're there for me.

God is Love

God is love.
Love is giving.
The purpose of living
is to live and love like royalty.

We share the kingdom of God
by simply being.

Love is communicated by vibration and frequency
because frequently, words get in the way
of clear spiritual seeing.

Love the energy.
Release the manifestation.

The truest proclamation of deep understanding
lies in the ability to articulate simplicity
with a smile,
with a dance,
acknowledging sweet synchronicity

with all that we see,
asking in every moment
what gift is being brought to me?

The Kite and the Rock

Beauty lies next to Wisdom in a familiar embrace,
old lovers who have danced through countless lifetimes.

Wisdom is the rock.
Beauty is the kite.

Beauty sways in the wind,
twirling in the elements
as lightning strikes,
removing layers from her face.

Wisdom burrows into Gaia,
breathing in and out,
keeping a slow and steady pace,
meeting all Beauty's dimensions with a warm smile,
he says,

I love you like this too.
I'm so grateful to witness this expression of you.
Every day you become more beautiful, boo.
You become more you.

Inner Jewels

Right now, I breathe deep.
Today, I move slow.
I relax and slowly re-enter the flow.

There's nowhere to get to
and no need to rush.

The jewels of my inner journey balance my wanderlust.

With my roots in the soil,
I grow towards the sky,
My spirit soars breezily as it learns to take flight.

Heart-centered Living

Eternal life
or unending strife,
the choice is yours to make.

The path to freedom begins
when you focus on what you can give
instead of what you can take.

Dijon Bowden

The Jubilation of Self-realization

With great jubilation
I revise the path of this incarnation
with crystalline clarity.

I devote myself to joyous integrity
by identifying the energy I leak
and carefully choosing the words I speak into existence.

Into existence intention blooms into action.

This self-realization produces heartfelt satisfaction
of soul longings made manifest
through consistency of connective practice.

Space is carved out for inspiration to flow freely
in ever widening swaths of serendipity.

Made in the image of our Creator,
I ignite my divinity now, not later.

True Love Aligns

Today, true love aligns
because we're in a field beyond time,
we're outside of mind.

A fresh start in the heart's dimension,
fantastically free,
nothing to tear us apart,
no separation,
just sweet sensation,
succumbing to temptation,
we surrender.
Remember

REMEMBER
blue days in December,
thawed out by elation and transcendent splendor.
Seasons change.
Now spring is here.
We're miles apart but I feel you near,
souls intertwined in an eternal dance,
a cosmically created operatic prance.
Our flame of friendship
ignites into communion with a touch of romance.

Cerebellum's Cage

How quickly we forget
the lessons of our lives,
the trappings of our minds,
the things that keep us blind.

So let us not forget
the calling of our souls,
the things that make us whole,
union with spirit our only goal.

The time for truth is now.
Devotion to God the how.
One with the eternal Tao.
Devotion to God the how.

Awaken with Grace

The love you gave so tenderly
suited me splendidly.
It awoke my heart
and unlocked the door to my cage.

Once free, I sprang forth joyfully
out of a sea of misery
into the start of a new phase.

Thank you for waiting patiently.
I finally released the shame and the rage.
I started a new chapter by accepting what is
and gracefully turning the page.

Pure Presence

Inspired by the beauty of breath,
I immortalize my essence,
eternal being awakened by reverent atonement.

The point where spirit meets matter
is also known as the present moment.

Illusions

Be conscious
of the illusion of power
while the ones that pull the strings
sit hidden away in jewel encrusted towers.

It's the illusion of choice
that has everyone bemused.
Until you see reality for what is really is,
you will stay confused.

Deeper realities exist inside yourself.
It's up to you to find them.

Meditation unlocks tremendous wealth.
Devotion will keep you shining.

Freedom lies within your reach,
if true liberation is what you seek.

The meek will RISE as the greedy fall.

Heart-centered living
gracefully awakens us all.

Faultline

Pain is your teacher.
Pain is your friend.
Pain shows you where your healing needs to begin.

Heartbreak is a gift.
Heartbreak helps you grow.
You end heartbreak by remembering the things you already know.

For love does not contain pain,
that is jealousy, expectation, and need.
Love is without limits and is given unconditionally.

Surrender your mind, and the days of separation are through.
Awaken and recognize everything you need is already within you.

Portals and Pathways

Pain is a pathway to transformation.
Glide through the portal to pure presence.

Your purpose is that which brings you at once
into ecstatic joy and deep peace at the same time.

II

Fluorescent Waves

Suffering catalyzes the transformation.
It took you leaving for me to release the fantasy of us.
Disillusionment sets me free
to embrace reality.

This is a complete life.
It's up to me to see it.
God is buried inside.
It's up to me to be it.

I realize my self-imposed strife.
I remember I am whole.
Illumination is balance,
riding waves to my eternal soul.

Looking inward provides relief
as we tune in to universal frequencies.
We now begin to find release
moving from infinity to infinity.

ARCTURUS

Gazing at the stars under a crescent moon,
our journey came to an end much too soon.
We bent time and spun finite moments into eternity,

delightfully devouring delicious delicacies.
The chocolate cake was bittersweet
as we prepared our hearts to part ways.

I imagined the mint tea to be laced with your essence,
heating my center from the inside out.
I decided no matter where the road led,
I would always carry you within me.

Spirits' Kiss

Truth is Truth,
there is no need to fear it.
God is love.
Bliss is soul meeting spirit.

Let go,
exhale,
there is no way to fail.

Stand tall.
Rise above.
Maintain your devotion to love.

Essence

Love has many faces.
You experience what you are.
Learn to see the essence beneath the surface.

Ripe Fruit

There is an interconnected interplay between
dark and light,
night and day,
rest and play.

The dreams your fear once delayed
are ripe for the picking today.

Balanced conscious choice
unlocks guarded gateways
to pristine portals and purposeful pathways.

Young Soul

Rise up.
Stay awake.
Stay clear, young soul.
Treasures await you far richer than silver and gold.

Emanations of divinity long to dwell within you,
activating your cells and enhancing nature's smells.
Can you keep opening despite everything you have to go through?

Just as an acorn is reorganized and transmuted to make an oak tree,
you will undergo deep metamorphosis to finally be free.

Nothing you know now will remain
and yet, there's something within that will always be the same,
something that gives life and animates your veins.

The one constant in all the change.

A NEW PATH

I dream about the freckle on the upper left side of your back
and the smell of your hair
and envision myself
tracing the lines of your body with my fingertips.

I still desire to come into contact with your flesh,
but now I relish the energy of your heart
and connecting to your mind in our telepathic tango.

The elation I feel is spiritual,
elevation beyond the physical.

The multi-tiered dimensional exploration
through planes of existence
produces tears of joy as we practice abstinence.
Not eternally, because passionate union grounded in God
is the molding of Heaven and Earth,
but until the foundation is solid
so as not repeat mistakes made since birth:
rushing into connection seeking relief from life's ills,
wanting you to be my soma pill,
enmeshing my power for unearned thrills.

I stand here, clear beyond patience,
with presence to this beautiful unfolding
as this path is one I've never walked before,
a journey of truth, respect, true love, and more.

Sorrow's Sting

Heartbreak is happiness inverted.
Your essence is underneath the emptiness.

Allow the torrent of tears to wash away grief
and fertilize tomorrow's transcendent art.

Awaken to the gifts change brings
while surrendering the misery of sorrow's sting.

Virgin Snow

Death is the greatest act of creation.
Every rebirth an act of transformation,
the old falling away,
making space for fresh life today.

Every savasana is a letting go
of thoughts formed long ago.
We are reborn in fetus,

fresh and pure like virgin snow,
incandescently illuminated.
As above,
so below.

Let Go

Life,
what a sweet gift.

Some part of me longs to be free,
one piece of the whole
out of control but in tune with the soul
and blessed unconditionally.

You can graciously give it away
or it can be painfully ripped from you one day.

But in the end, you must learn to let go,
trust,
breath out,
and remember what you already know.

Illumination

Enlightenment is not a completion point.
Life is constant change and eternal evolution.
Enlightenment is an inflection point,
an influx of the infinite light of your inner being into your body,
an infusion of subtle energies
that lessens the density of the matter that you call you.

Devotion

Descending into happiness feels freeing and fresh,
feet on the ground,
body and spirit enmeshed.
Despite detachment, flowers glisten in the sun.
This new dimension invites me to creativity, play, devotion, and fun.

Life is simple,
I know this to be true.
It's about slowing down,
connecting with Source within
to channel your truth.

Grateful for the opportunity to begin again,
rooted in self, I'm now my own best friend.

I honor all reflections of service,
for in creative service, I practice divine worship.

Rainbow Muse

In the place beyond time,
divine mind weaves rhymes.
Perfect prose and poetry flows,
spoken by the lips of Brahma.

From a pregnant silence springs
a kaleidoscopic spectrum of vibration,
descending in density
from ether to matter.

Harmony and joy reign
until Maya and Avidya stain
the multifaceted muse of creation.

Immortality regained
and order sustained
through stillness and silence in meditation.

Law of Attraction

Fear pulls something towards you.
Wanting something pushes it away.

Will you practice equanimity
as you consciously create your day?

Russian Roulette

Shiny lights flash
as the wheel of samsara spins
in playful games of chance.

As we explore the gambler's dance,
there is an extraordinary opportunity
to overcome the waves of fear and greed.
Stay unattached to outcome to be free.
The game is only as serious as you make it out to be.

Ambrosia

The irony of rushing to eternity tickles me.
What will you do when you get there?

Divinity in ubiquity
is everything that you seek
and why is it you resist?

Where do you head off to
when you drift to the dance of the world?
Can you release distraction?
Cultivate joy and satisfaction,

embrace the gift of the present,
and lie in the field of forever,
tantalized by the taste of the nectar of apricot ambrosia?

Allow the bud of spirit
to bloom within your bosom,
melting away disillusionment from your days.

God's love is here,
holding you dear
now and forever.

Soul Science

You are magnificent,
at once a single nanoparticle
and the entire quantum field,

a fraction and the whole.
Does this ring true
when you tune in to the call of your soul?

The truth is always there,
cosmic creativity beneath circumstantial despair.

Feel the vibrations kickstart your heart
as remembrance envelops your being
while sliding into a warm bath on a cool autumn evening.

A Field of Jasmine

Rest easy,
you've always been free.
Feel the love of the grass and the trees
while you lie in a field of jasmine.

Taste the sweet juice from a peach
as you remember you already have that which you seek.
The earth, your mother, provides all that you need.

The challenges you face seeking love
invite you to look within to harvest a cornucopia of connection.

Change your choices.

Be not a beggar of love.
You are the gatekeeper.
Claim your self worth.
Embrace your rebirth.
Free yourself from invisible chains.
Remember and activate full violet flame.

Harmony

Cycles end gracefully.
New beginnings start playfully
and the whole universe sings along.

Infinite joy cultivated internally,
harvesting the fruit of life eternally,
aligning with nature's silent song.

In gratitude, I bow to the gifts grace has given,
gifts which have molded me into the man I've become.
Something new and ancient within has risen,
SURRENDER transforming inner cacophony into knowing all is one.

III

Reverence

Orange peels and olive trees,
mint tea and verbena leaves,
secret doorways opened with ease
by dropping respectfully to your knees.

Gratitude given and connections made,
blessings received and foundations laid
for new beginnings
and graceful endings.

The sun rises and trees sway.
Illuminate as you meditate,
it's a brand-new day.

Poppies and Lavender

Shine,
and let the warmth from your own heart heal your soul.
Shine,
and let yourself sing without self-consciousness.
Shine,
and dance yourself free in fields of grass
peppered with poppies and lavender.

Kneel, and know the answers you seek
are waiting on you to stop searching
to be still so they can reveal their mysteries
in an eloquent unraveling of wonder.
Place your bare feet on the earth to commune with your mother.
Breathe in fresh air purified by the trees.
Feel the wind tickle the hairs on your neck.

There are secrets in the dimensions of the air,
air that carries spiritual current into your body,
your temporary home for your soul's journey through this realm.

The lesson is to let go of the destination,
to awaken to the truth that
that which you seek already lives within you,
waiting to be activated by your pure presence.

When your yearning for yoga with the divine
saturates your consciousness,
reflections of holy union
will rocket forth into your holographic experience,
opening your heart to everything spirit brings in your path.

Alchemy

To alchemize the gold inside you,
consistent conscious cultivation
of your spiritual frequency is key.
Incrementally increase your base vibration
to connect with eternity.

Meditate, elevate, integrate
the blueprint to connect you to the field beyond time.
Celebrate your awakened state
as a joyful reflection of divine mind.

Remembrance

Abundance comes from being aligned with source.
Let go of your mind, control, and force.

You already are everything you seek.
When you remember that truth, you're free.

Hungry Ghosts

I still believe in joy,
but I'm done falling in love.

True love is not something that happens to you,
but a seed sprouting, shattering illusions
and transforming everything you do,

a river rushing, cleansing toxicity
and purifying everything in you.

Magic erupts when you unexpectedly connect
with a soul that reflects your multi-dimensionality.
This is certainly special, but it is not love.

It'd be more accurate to say metaphysical chemical combustion.

It is a spark, a jumpstart to your heart,
an oasis in a desert making you feel less alone,
but not necessarily love.

Be wary of feeding the hungry ghost within you with just anything.
Practice patience.
Discern if the meal being offered is true nourishment
or the newest trendy diet.

True love is a choice.
It's devotion to hearing someone's true voice,
to learning their weaknesses,
to holding compassionate space,
to honoring their autonomy and not trying to save or fix them.

True love is a giving enaction,
not an empty transaction.

True love begins within,
in a devotional dance with spiritual friends,
moving cyclically towards eternity.

So, in joy, I choose true love.
I choose merging with the stars above.
I choose prioritizing my spiritual and physical health
and ritualistic deepening of self.

Timeless Love

You can be in love all the time.

It's a choice.

People will come and go,
but you can keep them in your heart.

You can drift into a new planetary orbit
and still exist within the same solar system.
The heart is infinite and, when you keep it open,

you allow yourself to access
ever increasing feelings of joy, bliss, and fulfillment.

Dijon Bowden

The Farmer and the Peach

Today I fantasized about being a farmer.
The pride of my garden was a precious peach tree.
Day by day I sat out in the shade of its leaves,
studying the delicate fruit.
I named the most vibrant piece after you.
My loving gaze accelerated your maturation.
My happiness found in placing fresh fertilizer at your roots
and watching you dance in joy
as the wind stroked the fuzz on your skin.
Sometimes I stayed with you all night.

I sang songs to you under the moonlight
and chanted mantras in the morning at sunrise.
I knelt in prayer, witnessing the miracle of life
until I fell asleep in the grass under the tree.

When I awoke, you were lying gingerly on my chest,
so perfectly ripe that you had fallen off of the tree
in offering, ready to be relished.
I prayed to spiritualize the blessing and slowly bit
into your soft, supple flesh.
Your juices ran down my chin
as I burrowed my lips into your lusciousness.
I wasn't just satiated solely in body, but also in mind and soul.
The union between us
produced something transcendent, jubilant, and whole.

Divine Vibrations

Music is the language of the divine,
odorless, invisible, and intangible
but omnipresent.

Vibrations swirl through the ether,
waiting for a receptive vessel.

The worthy recipient brings forth worlds for people to dance in,
setting the stage for new romance to begin,
allowing the deepest grief relief,
enveloping tones, replacing the feeling of being alone.

A beautiful connective tool,
mysterious, fiery, calming, and cool.

Discipline

The castle of your consciousness
is illuminated by consistency.

Free from Sin

Fear not, dear child,
there is no such thing as sin.
Hell only exists when you try to fill yourself from the outside in.

Infinite possibilities are available to you
when you let down your walls and honor your truth.

Eternity is in the moment.
Your joy lights the path back home.
Breathe in peace.
Breathe out Om.

Your heart radiates love and reveres simplicity,
practicing presence as life moves towards unrivaled unity.

God is unconditional love,
always rooting for you to win.
Will today be the day
you start the journey with no beginning and no end?

Distractions

Choose compassion when facing fractures in your mind,
warring factions inventing distraction
to keep you from sacred silence.

Meditate on the taste of a peach,
the purity of snow.

Realize the wisdom of surrender,
the joy of letting go.

Remember the infinite power of your wondrous soul
as it recognizes its place in the infinite ever-expanding whole.

Ancient Ancestors

What is buried beneath those roots?
Memories upon memories.
Are we scared to feel the blues?
For centuries and centuries.
Can we awaken cosmic truth
of the multiverse and galaxy?

There are things that become true
when we can simply be.

I remember you.
It's good to see you again.
How have you been,
my old friend?

Relax into being.
You are the eternal observer.
Third eye awakening,
love what is with fervor.

Dijon Bowden

The Rhythm of Flow

There are many roads.
Some wander looking for direction,
holographic illusions
elicit projection.

All paths lead to the pearly gates.
Cultivate depth, not speed,
and heaven awaits.

Options can be taken away,
but never your power of choice.
Trust your intuition
and your soul will rejoice.

Unplug

Freedom means being active on multiple dimensions.
Traverse the 3D world and illuminate the imagination.
Access ascension with keys found in an inner sanctum,
and the possibilities of exploration are boundless.

Rise by unplugging from the limiting frequencies that surround us.
Spirit's voice within is where we place our trust.
Organic food and nature's wisdom will save us.

Rejuvenation

Today I rest
and that is okay.
You don't always have to have something profound to say.

You tend to the body
and allow yourself peace.
Release the momentum,
let all movement cease.

You begin again,
when you feel compelled to.
If you practice conscious death,
life more easily flows through.

Keys to Awakening

Proceed through a portal of purity
to enjoy a pathway of peace.
Forego the five sense trappings,
your sixth sense lights the avenue of ease.

Vibratory currents are illuminated by frequency.
Forego the mind to truly be free.
Intuition speaks in whispers to your heart.
Master the inhalation of breath
to make your entire life art.

Awaken your soul
to the gift of now.
Presence is the key,
gratitude the how.

Astrally Attuned

Grateful for the healing forgiveness brings,

heart full from the soothing songs spirit sings,

the divine rejoices because I create space for attunement,

slowing down to savor the moment's movement,

knowing love is always here

and, where there is perfect love,

there is no fear.

Love's power to heal inspires me

to radiate peace, joy, power, and tranquility.

Heavens' Gate

You can experience heaven at any time
because this ocean blue oasis is not based on external circumstances
but rather on internal perception.

Dijon Bowden

Smooth Sandpaper

The texture of my tears
washes away hidden fears
as they caress my cheeks
and release buried grief.

When all emotion has run its course,
I fully experience the present,
tapping into its source.

No projection into the future
nor nostalgia for the past,
I am free to exist
at peace at long last.

Debt Free

When you're teetering on the edge of expansion,
slicing away addiction's constrictive tendrils,
what matters is that you slow down,
contemplate,
be profoundly pensive.

If something costs you your peace,
it's too expensive.

ICARUS

As the wax melts from around my anointed feathers,
all delusions and stories cease.

I pray for perpetual peace.
Peace of mind,
Peace within our hearts,
Peace to calm our darkest thoughts.

It is done
It is done
It is done

Rapid, consistent elevation
fueled by rays of the glistening summer sun.

Your Child

Dear God,

I have so much fear in me.
I have been removing distraction,
feeling my attraction towards you
but am scared to surrender.

It's just your ego, they say,
and that may be true,
but I need you, Lord,
please take this fear from my heart.

Allow me to rest in your love and grace.
Show me your face in a way I can receive.

I am your child.
I release these wild times,
these days of supposed fun,
these confused incarnations.

I am ready to heal.
I am ready for what's real.
Help me surrender.
Help me kneel.

Homecoming

It has taken me a while to slow down,
to stop the compulsions to do,
to embrace being a human being
doing nothing,

sitting here watching the trees sway,
their leaves glistening in the sunlight,
the rays warm the side of my face.
I close my eyes and the corners of my mouth
turn up in a smile.

The speed of nature teaches us so much.
Vibration is the universal language.
Consciously curating your frequency
gives you the keys to the entire universe.

Dijon Bowden

The heart field moves slow and steady,
not rushing towards anything
and not pushing anything away.
Full in and of itself,
ready to meet any visitor like an old friend,
no matter how many times we leave its house,
we can always slow down,
breathe deep
and return home again.

IV

Pollination

You are a spider,
creating home from within,
attracting all you need to you,
your journey to sovereignty begins.

You are a lotus flower,
your lover a honeybee,
release your scented heat
and your king will share their seed.

You are a dog with no reservations.
You are simple and free.
Existing only in the present moment,
you practice love unconditionally.

Lemurian Love

I pray for your joy,
for your heart to feel whole,
for the desires of your body
to align with the healing of your soul.

In gratitude, I say farewell
as you adventure and explore.
This chapter concludes,
giving way to splendor.

We are always connected,
two leaves on a tree,
radiant raspberry redwoods
whose roots run deep.

Dijon Bowden

Thank you for the reflections.
Your heart is pure tropical water,
clear as quartz crystal,
and strong like a spider's web,
delicate and ornate.

Thank you for helping me remember
that salvation lies in showing up for service.

A New Start

Sitting in silence is quality time with the sublime.
Asana inhabits the body, freeing us from the mind.
Combine them for a timeless experience of the divine
for, in ultimate reality, there is no time.

Practice presence while brushing your teeth.
You have the power to give yourself relief.
You are your own healer,
your own guru,
your own best friend.

Every moment in life is a chance to begin again.

Dijon Bowden

The Universe Chose Us

The ocean sways in harmonious waves
as we celebrate this beautiful day,
gently kissed by the sun's rays,
we sing and dance and laugh and play.

As we connect within returning home
we know in our hearts that we're never alone.
We pause to remember that we are blessed.
We inhale ease and exhale stress.

We birth the new Earth
with peace, love, joy, and trust.
The time is now.
The Universe Chose Us.

Medjool Dates

The stem of a lilac,
the tangerine sky,
everything radiates beauty
when viewed through clear eyes.

The sweetness of a date,
the healing essence of a rose
and apricot infused tea
unravel my woes.

Primed to spin freely,
I embrace what's here now.
I surrender completely,
to the divine within I bow.

My spirit rejoices with new excitement to live.
I release thoughts of future fulfillment
and focus on what I can give.

Twin Flame

Everything aligns
in perfect rhyme
when you surrender to the field beyond time,
to the divinity beyond mind,
as the secret serpent slithers up your spine.

Insecurities and fears melt away
when she truly sees you and you embrace.

It began from within,
the healing that you feel
because, at the deepest level,
relationship with self
is the only thing that's real.

She is a reflection
of the love you've found inside.
Keep burrowing inward
as outwardly you become more alive.

You're primed to share your gifts,
the fruits you've cultivated are ripe.
Realize the ancient Arcturian myths.
You are an intergalactic warrior of light.

Conscious Creator

Life is happening to you;
you are a victim.

Life is happening for you;
you are awakening.

Life is happening through you;
you are in communion.

Dijon Bowden

Blanket of Light

The warmth of the sun's rays
caresses my soul like an exquisite lover.

The hum of car engines as they shuffle by,
peppered by the tooting of horns,
the symphony of sensation paints an operatic backdrop
for the dance of two golden butterflies frolicking in the sunlight.

Succulents stand sturdy beneath their flight.
The leaves of baby palm trees rustle as the wind whistles by.

In my heart and mind, I know I finally see with clear eyes.
I am blessed, kissed by the lips of God,
at one with the cosmos,
with a playful nod to illusory façade,
free to rest in the self,
free to break free,
free to walk the heart's path eternally.

Celestial Captain

Through the ups and downs,
I know that I am blessed.

Heavenly frequencies speak to me,
elevating me above worldly stress.

Angels whisper their siren songs

as I float through astral realms,
returning integrated,

resistance obliterated
as my soul takes the helm.

THE COSMIC RAY

Fear is nothing more than shallow breath.
Inhale deep to your core.

Let the breath massage your pelvic floor
and what's right will erase what's left.

Trust is a muscle you can develop.
Saturate your consciousness
in holy texts
and spirit will envelop your entire being.

Love is the emanation that transforms,
align with the cosmic ray to be reborn.
In childlike play you hide and seek,
on this magical day, your soul is free.

Balance Beam

If we're only here for a flash
and every day is a gift,
let us live in joy
and sorrow
without thought of tomorrow.

No, that doesn't mean there isn't morality
because that mentality produces imbalance in the moment
and the balanced moment is the way
to deeper levels of ease and play.

Paths wind and swirl in illusory curls,
heading nowhere but here
and Now
and the rhythm of the heart is the how,
the answer to all questions,
the final frontier, nothing less than

Peace.

Rebirth

Rivers run deep
oceans bleed blue
acorns hatch trees
soft morning dew

blazing hot ice
wet healing ground
shanti shanti Om
cosmically vibrating sound

The Womb

There is no goal.
The soul is leading you home
with its invisible glow

to a place even sweeter than the scent of her hair
as she rested her head on your chest
while you lay in bed
the first night you moved in together.

Dreaming of family,
she guided you to relax into release,
producing progeny with passion.

Home is a direction,
not a place or destination.
Your soul is lighting the way

to a feeling more familiar
than sitting in the living room watching football
while the scent of Granny's collard greens
waft into your nostrils on Thanksgiving Day.

Home is the NOW,
the how,
the womb of transformation.

Om is the primordial vibration of creation.
Chant it as mantra,
feel its reverberation.

Astral Aviation

When inward experience
outweighs external appearance,
you will transform and fly,
a bird humming here and there,
spreading joy everywhere,
steady like heat from the sun.

Above the clouds, your spirit soars.
You spread good tidings
and open doors
to higher pathways of prismatic light,
the air is clear at this rarefied height.

Sacred Ground

Forgiveness is the fertilizer that repairs soil made barren
by bitterness, anger, and judgment.
Invite the cooling waters of peace to refresh your soul
and end all duality.

There is no you, there is no me.
Complete clarity sees the reflections on the screen.

Know that the ultimate goal of being made whole
comes in complete surrender to God.
After your time to dance and play in these realms is complete,

you will return to your essence to rest in bliss.

Floating Ships

Release.
Let go.
Spirit provides all you need to know.

Give thanks.
Rejoice!
Suffering ends when you tune into God's voice.

True understanding pacifies your brain.
You regain your eternal being
when you consciously face your pain.
Maintain your devotion to awaken new seeing,

all fear eliminated with right thinking,
that sinking restlessness banished
as you soar into eternity like an eagle.

Divine Decadence

Breathe consciously,
letting the essence of the divine
caress the spaces between vertebrae
along your spine.

Eat mindfully,
savoring the sweetness of sacred sustenance
and the completeness
of pure-bred piquant romance.

Pray ceaselessly,
creating holiness in every moment
through your intention to simply be.

Royalty

Today is the celebration of a new birth,
a vast reservoir of self-love unearthed.
No longer bowing my head
to fit in with sheep,
the promises to my Self
are the ones that I keep.

The keys to awakening were found deep in the dark.
Gut-wrenching wounds were triggered to break open my heart.
Every toxic emotion concealed
a trauma to be witnessed, held, and healed.

Underneath layers of pain
was strength, clarity, and the unwritten rules of the game.
Forgiveness is one of the highest laws
that softens bitterness out of clenched jaws.

No longer carrying the weight of shame,
only my pure heart, ready to serve, remains.
I release all that does not honor me as King,
knowing a new age of harmony is the gift that I bring,
energy reserved for conscious creation,
channeling visionary art for the world's elevation.

Selfless

What will you make of this wondrous day?
The whole universe excitedly invites you to play.
The possibilities of expression know no limits.
Even though it's illusion, God longs to express pure love in it.

Will you be of service and open your heart?
It's a great remedy when things fall apart.
If you want to ascend and make your soul feel lighter,
focus on how you can make just one person's day brighter.

Starseed

This road has been so long
and yet, here I am.
Slowing down to deepen into the now,
you wouldn't believe the trials I have lived through
in order to heal my family line.
I signed up for this human journey
through three-dimensional space and time,
divine incarnation unfolding in dank darkness.

Every trauma is a gift,
grace buried inside struggle
like a sweet fruit hiding within a prickly shell,
the precious nectar only available to those with
perseverance and patience.

With deep resolve and dynamic volition not just to survive,
but to thrive in the face of despair,
I breathe in the scent of Shakti's hair,
and glide up the inner chamber of my double helix DNA.
Everything burned away
in the transformative fire of ludus, eros, and agape.

When I feel lost, I surrender to my knees,
knowing breath is my greatest friend, ally, and bringer of peace.

I find strength in my scars,
combining the human
with eternal being formed from the stars.

Tiny Totems

A hummingbird crossed my path on her way to a daisy.

Her wings shuttled levity into my soul.
She turned to face me and asked, "Where is your joy?"
I smiled and accepted the challenge to create it.

For what is enlightenment without exuberance?

Wasted potential crushes your spirit,
so now I vow to exercise it,
dancing divinity gleefully expressing infinity.

Oceanic Reflections

Breathe in,
it's time to begin again.

Breathe out,
there's nothing you can't live without.

All the things you love
are reflections from within.
Take refuge in the spirit
housed by your sensitive skin.

You were a prince,
riding a tidal wave.
Now you are waking up to the truth
that your senses kept you a slave.
Cravings, rooted in desire,
healed by connection to self.
Wisdom, awakened by fire,
you now possess a King's wealth.

Under Moroccan Skies

Under Moroccan skies,
I found peace.
The incessant worries about the future ceased.

Under Moroccan skies,
I was blessed.
The present moment proposed
and I said yes.

Under Moroccan skies, I found God.
When I caught eyes with strangers, they gave me a nod.
In those moments of transcendence, I knew
the reasons behind everything I had been through.

Before the radiant Light faded away,
he leaned in close with something to say—
he said, "In order to embody your truest self,
accept death and stop chasing wealth."

As the unconditionally loving sun set,
I knew this version of me was the best one yet.

About the Author

Dijon Bowden is a multi-dimensional artist who believes in self-actualization as a means to inspire others to ignite their own divinity. The meditation retreats and yoga teacher training he has attended have allowed him to sustain a powerful connection to Source energy and channel visionary art. Storytelling, music, poetry, photography, and filmmaking are vehicles he uses to share high vibrational healing energy. His musical project, *Indigo Keys*, creates cosmic soundscapes that are accompanied by cinematic visuals to create epic, soulful experiences that speak to the human heart and soul. His storytelling project, *SOULS of Society*, aims to create compassion, empathy, and spiritual awareness and has made millions of impressions online. *From Infinity to Infinity* is his first volume of poetry.

www.ingramcontent.com/pod-product-compliance
Lightning Source LLC
LaVergne TN
LVHW011845060526
838200LV00054B/4166